AF321599

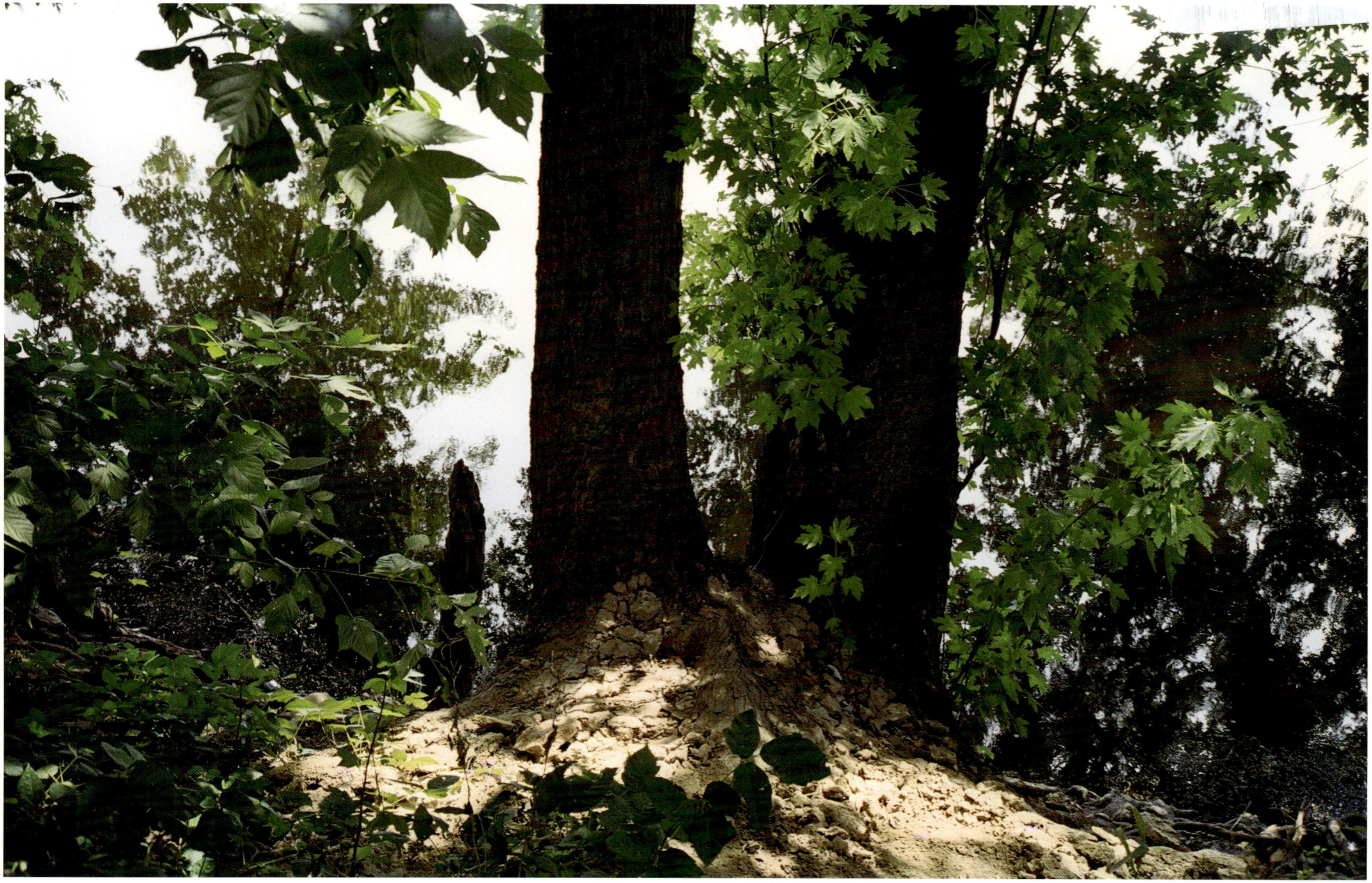

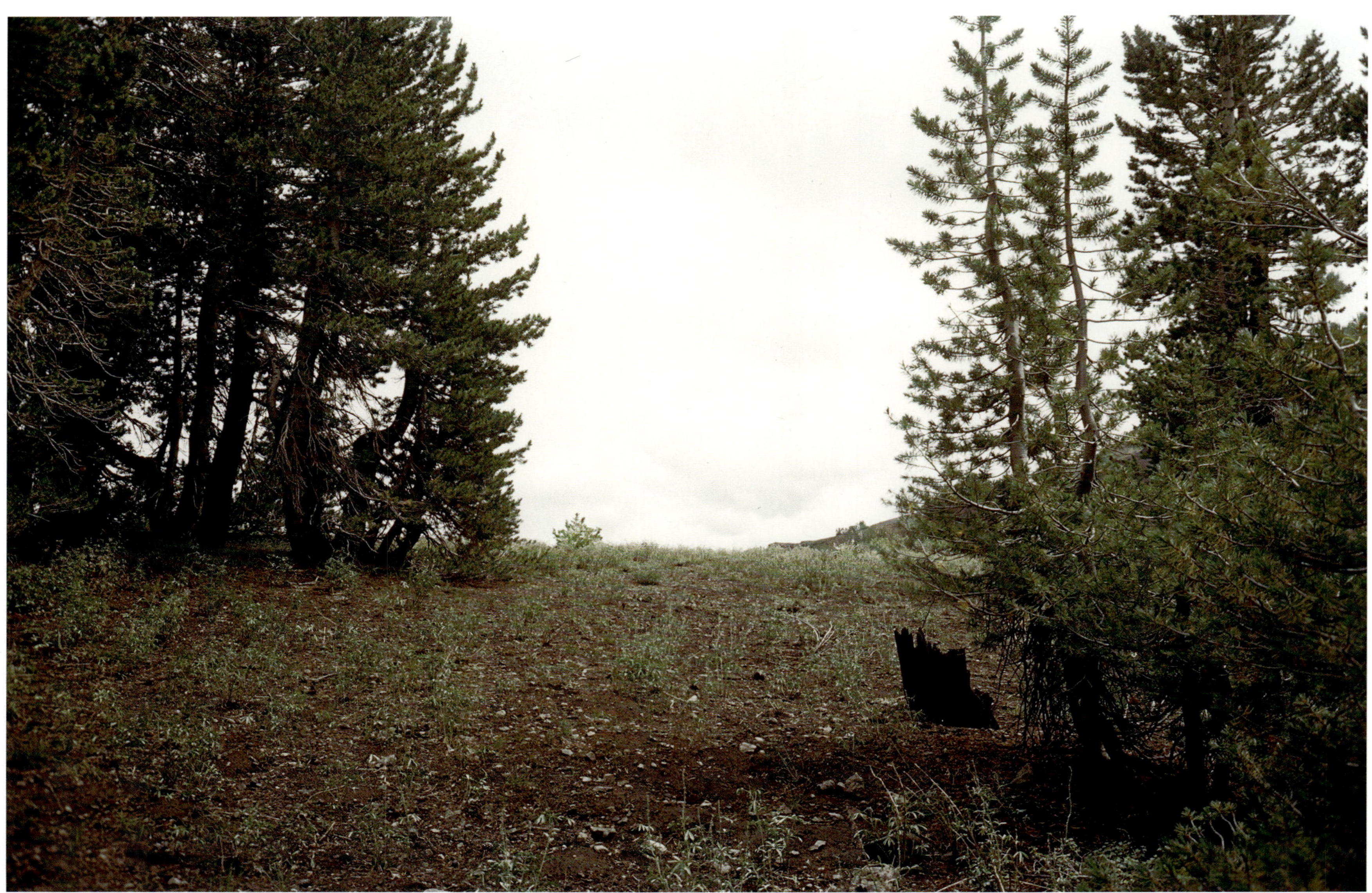

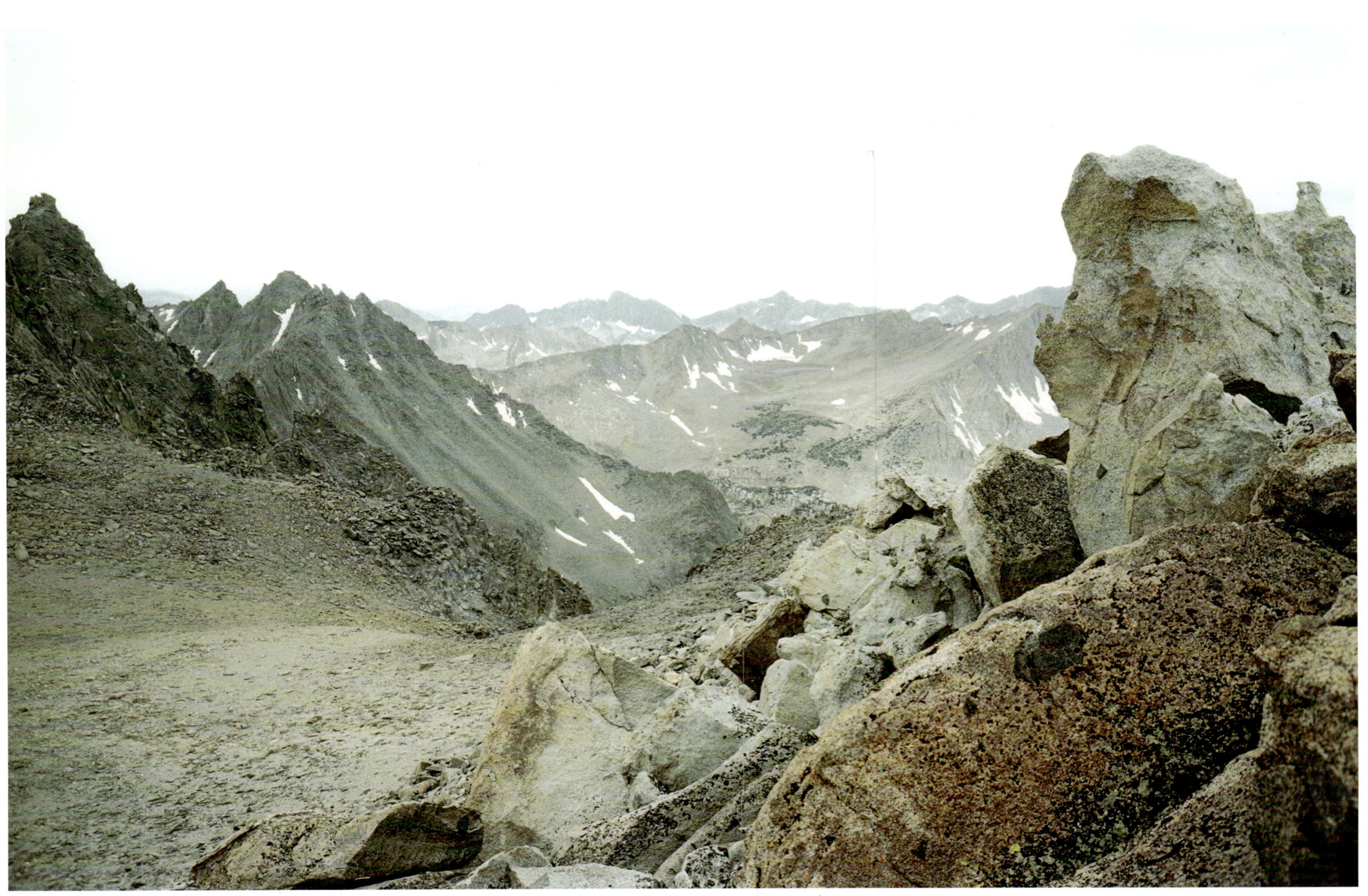

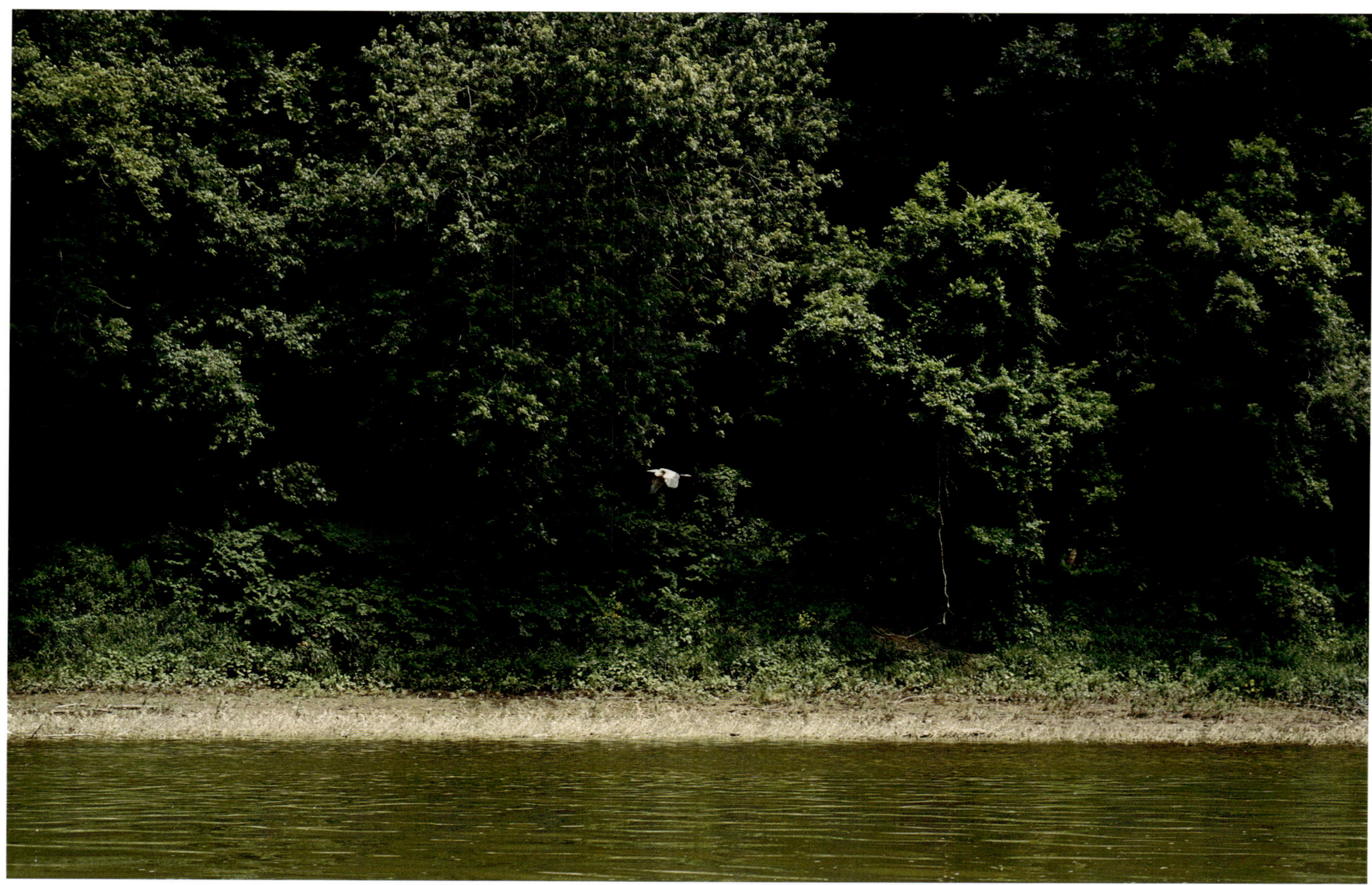

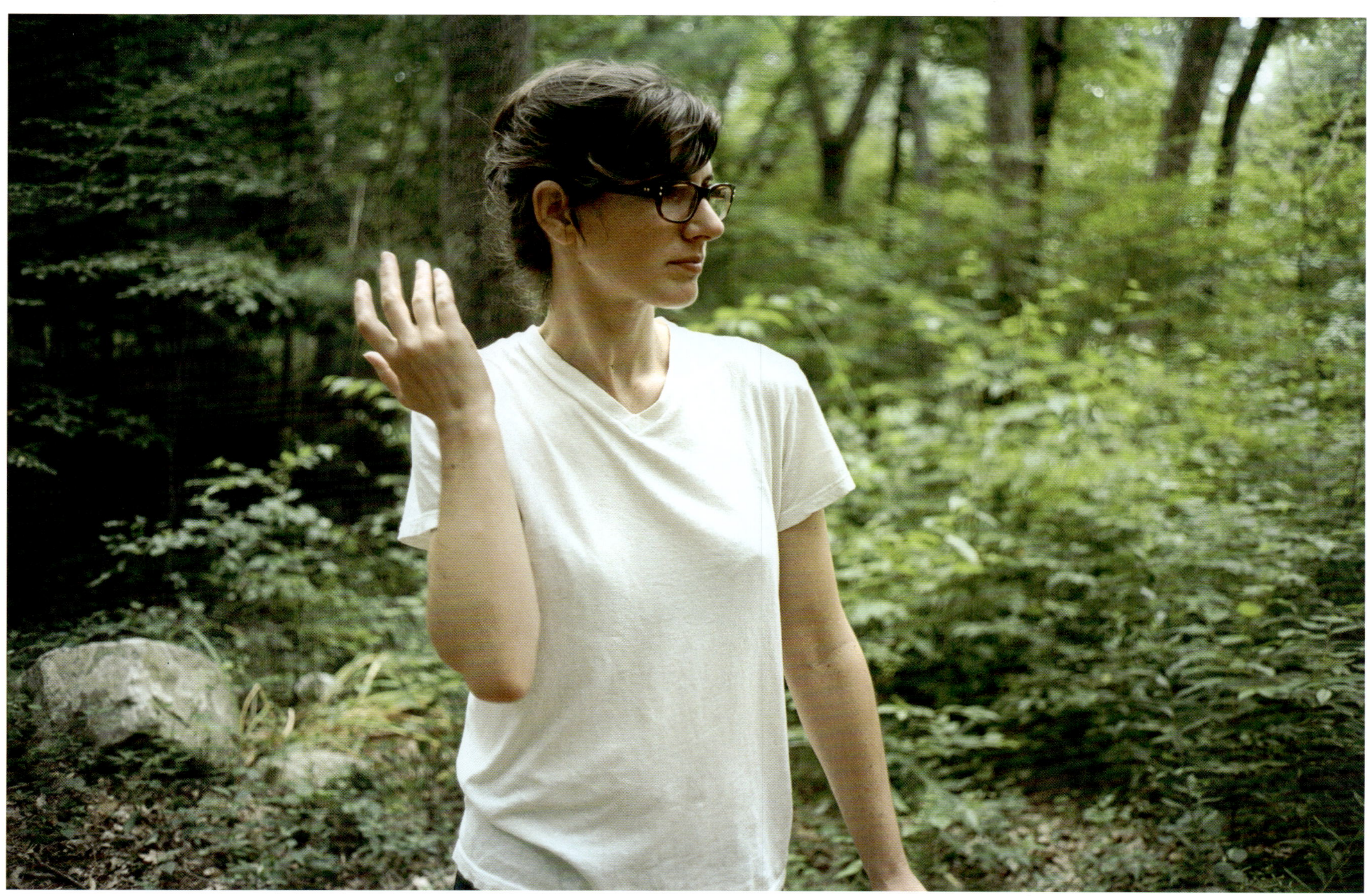

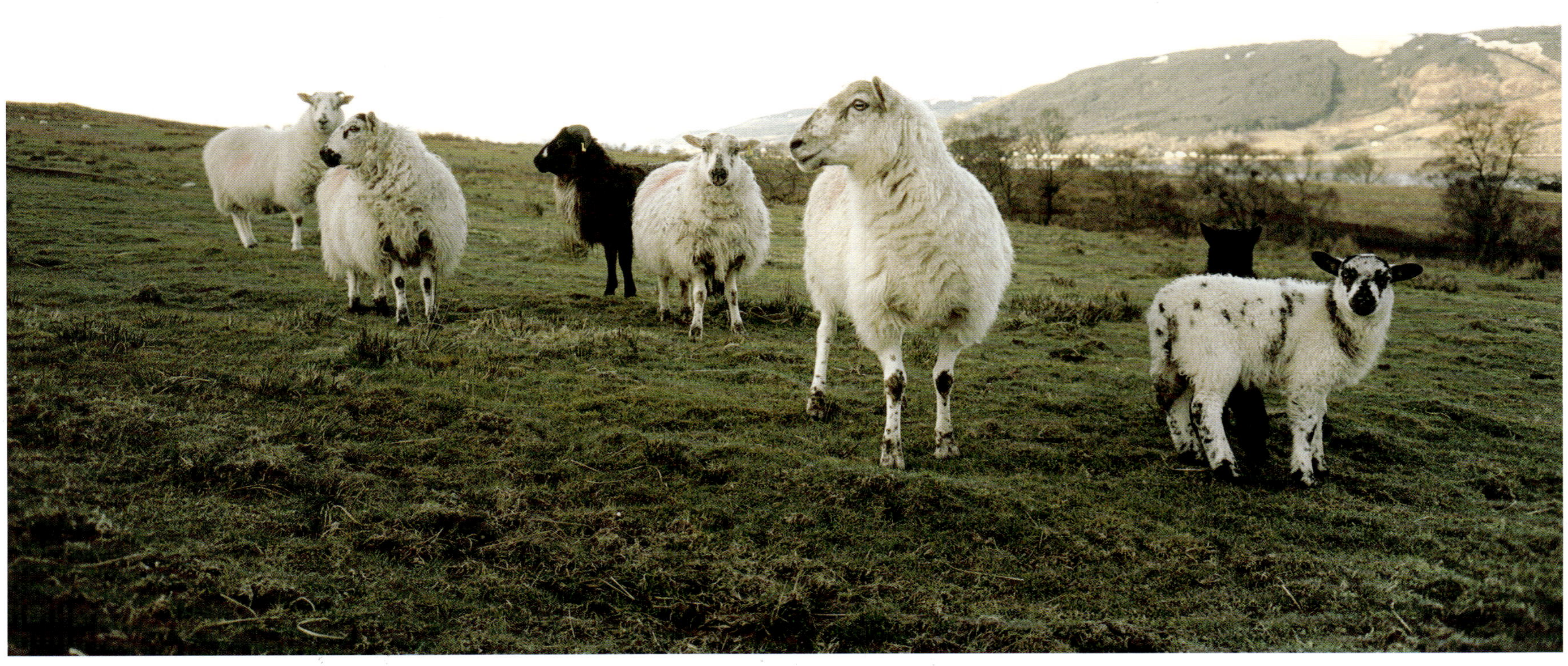

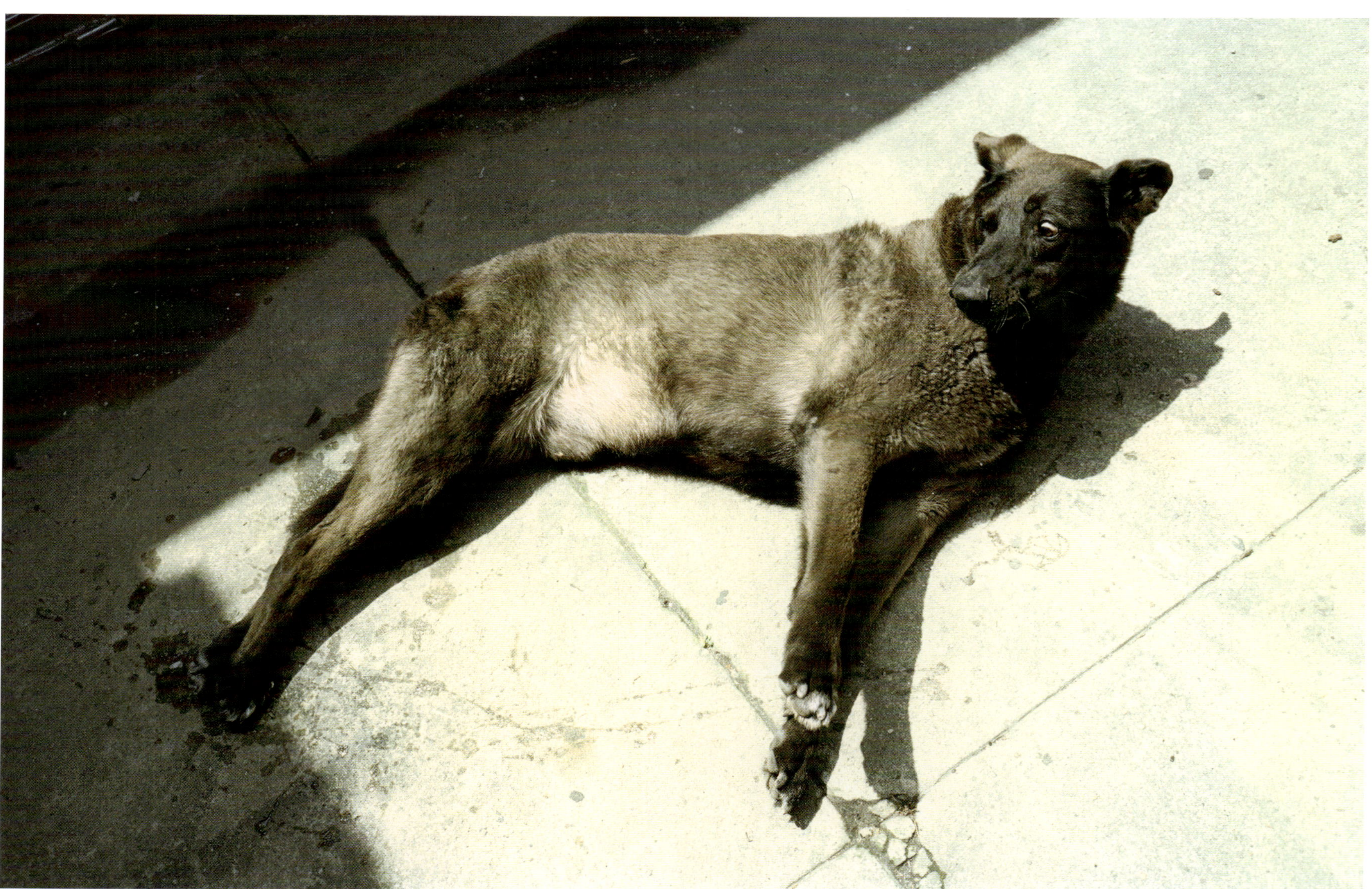

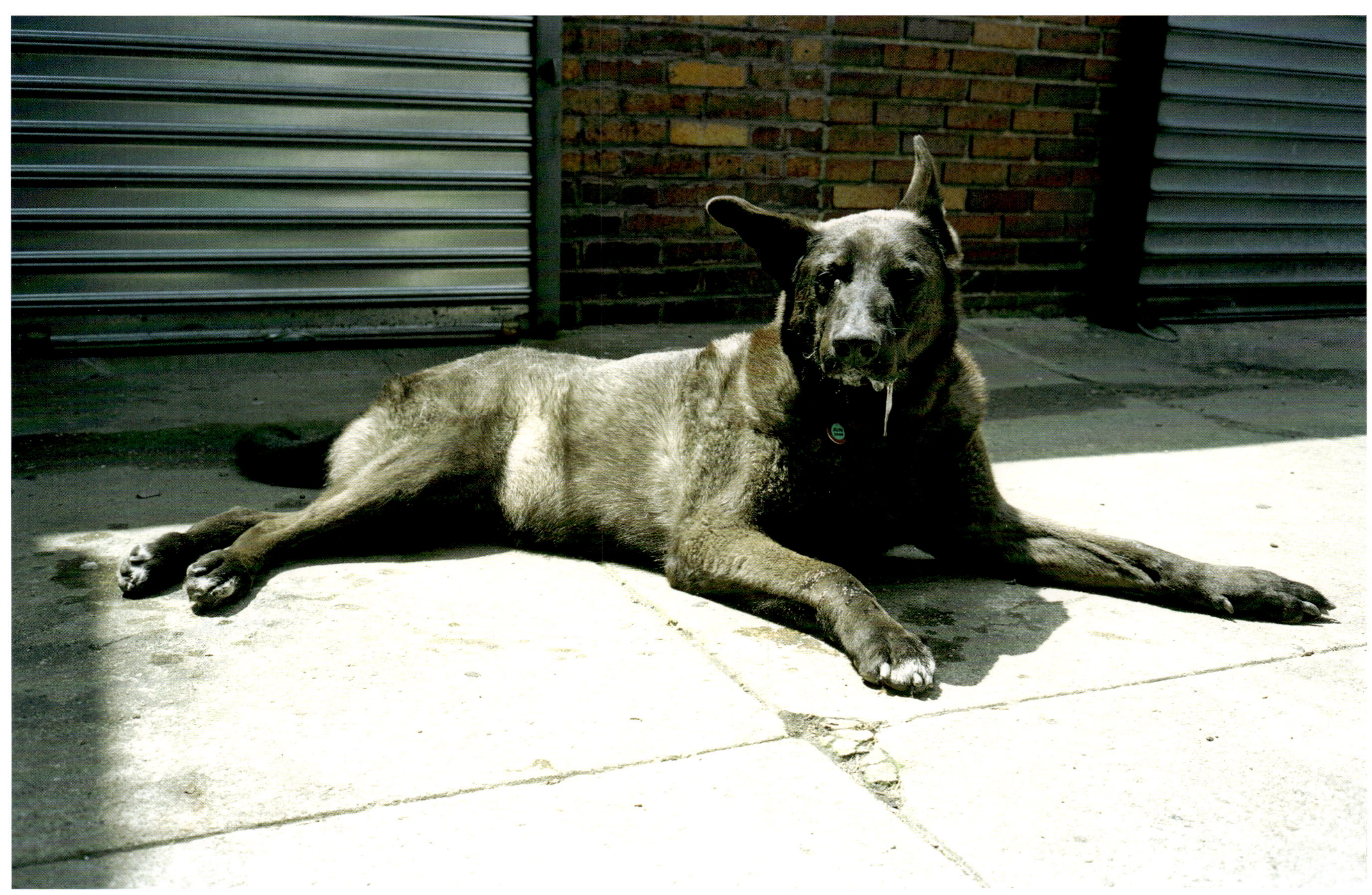

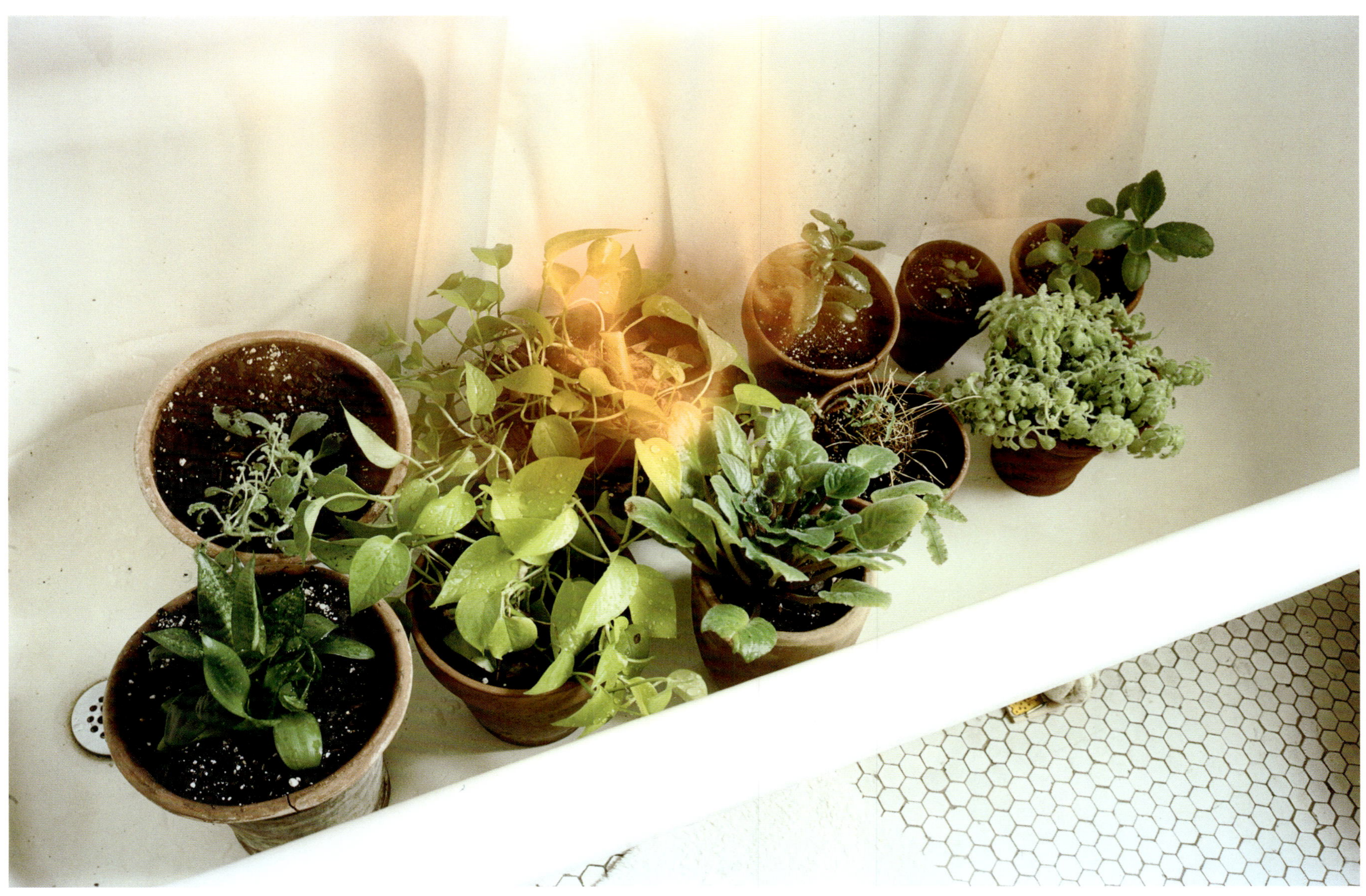

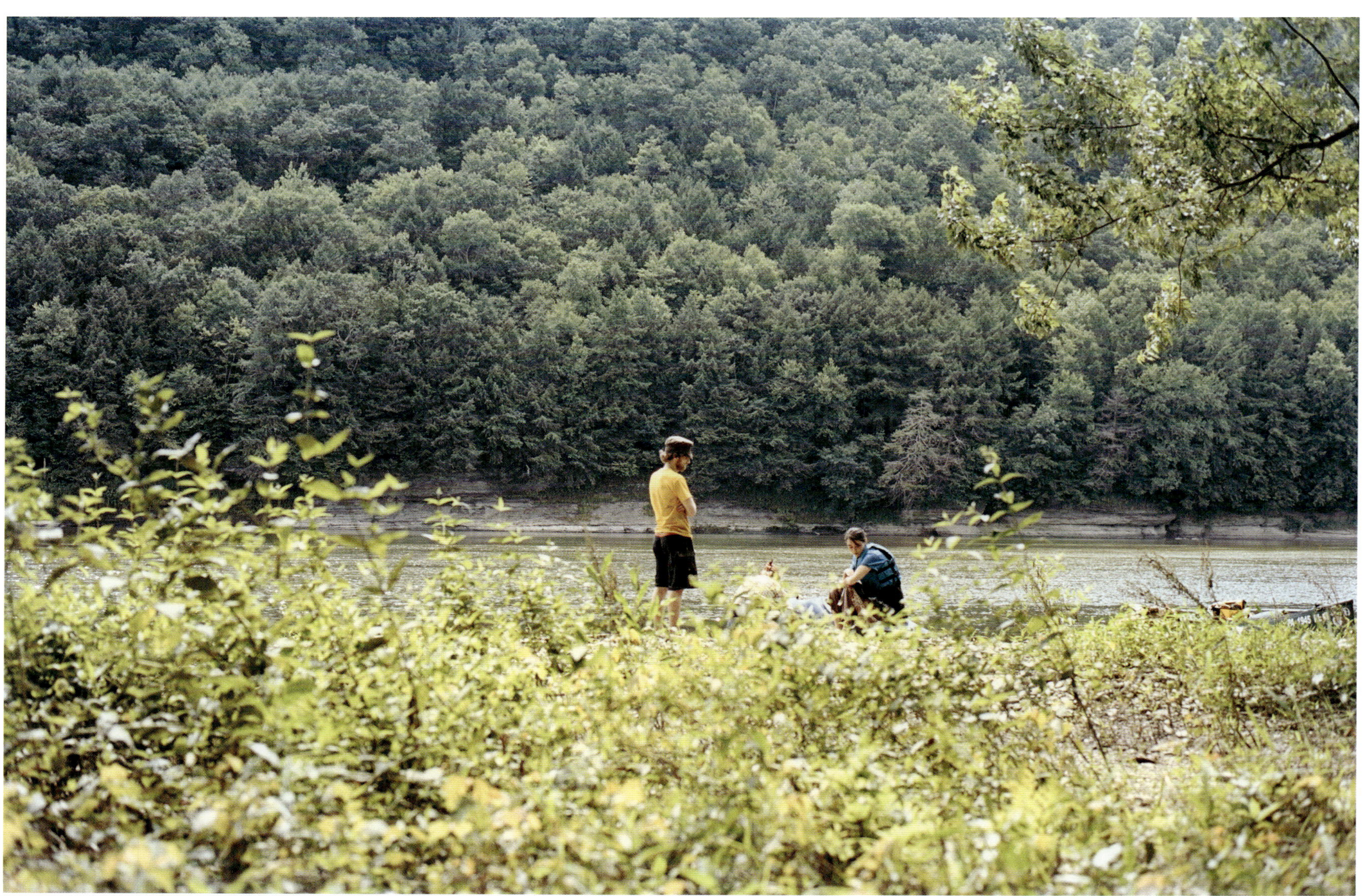

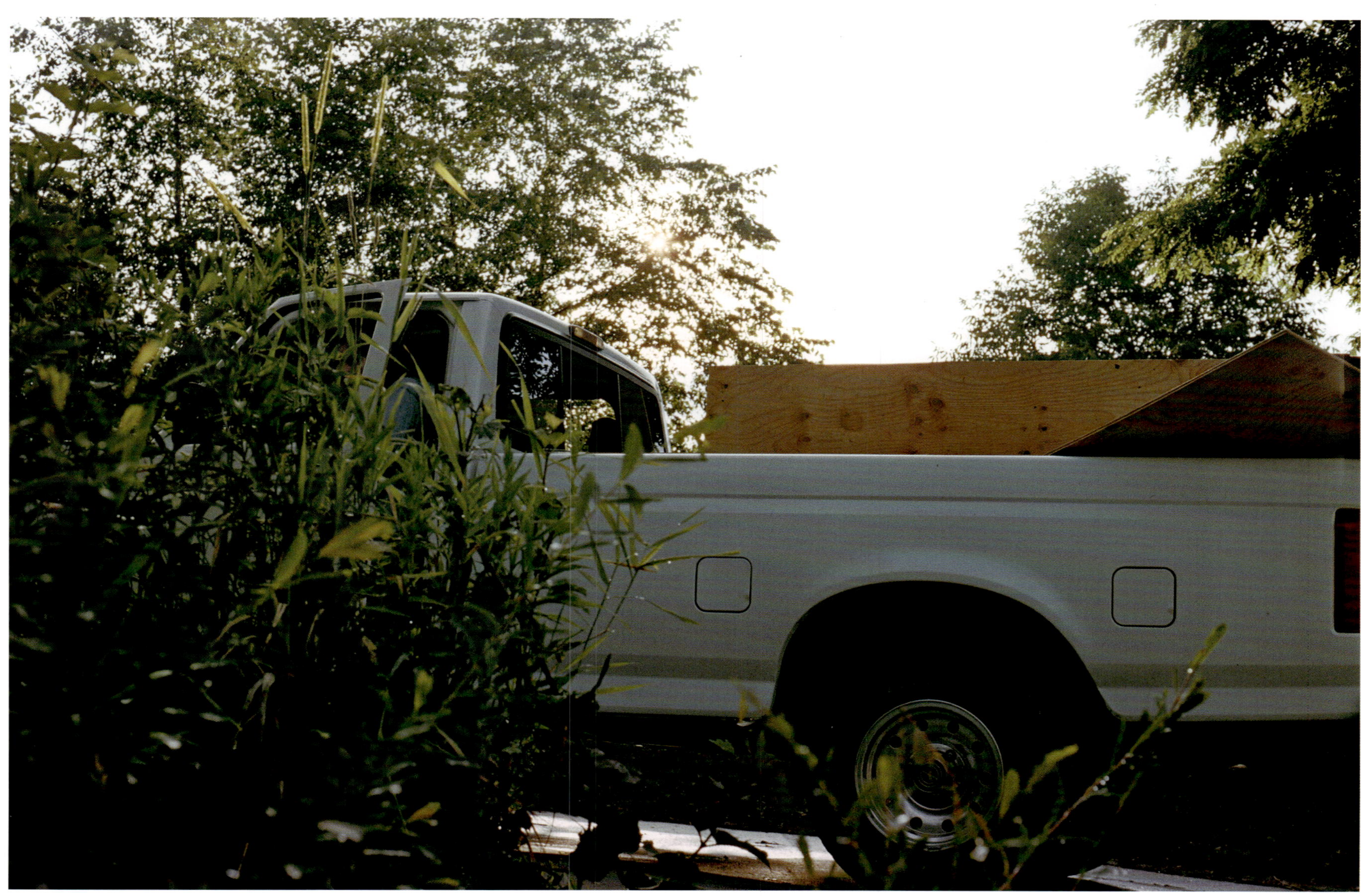

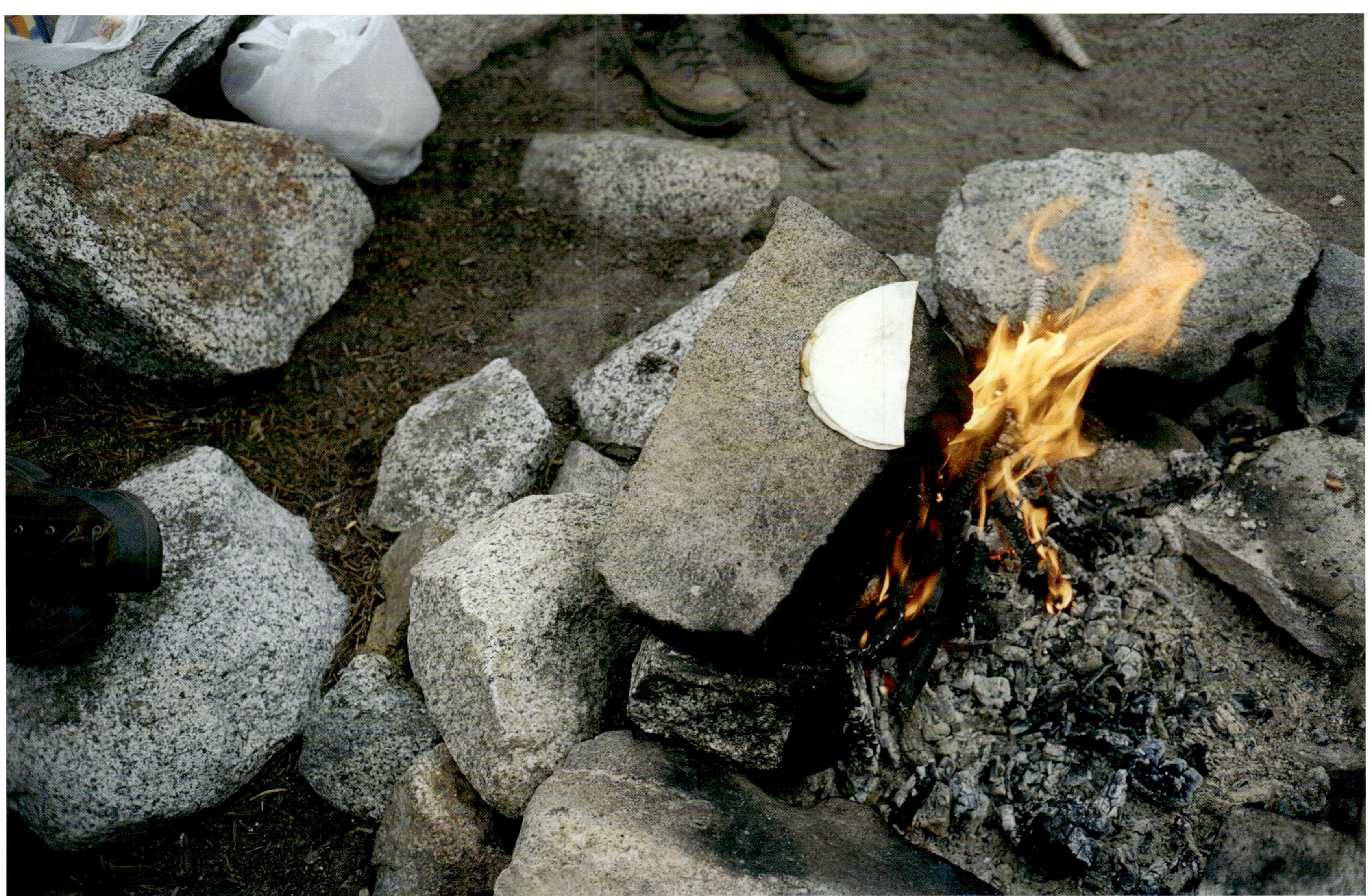

SKYDIVING
Publication © 2010 Dan Torop and A-Jump Books
Photographs © 2010 Dan Torop (2007-2009)

Published by A-Jump Books, Ithaca, NY
Printed by Eastwood Litho, Syracuse, NY
Edition of 500
First printing

ISBN 978-0-9777655-6-0

A-JUMP BOOKS
www.a-jumpbooks.com
info@a-jumpbooks.com

Point of Rocks, 2007

Pass, 2009
Vagabond Peak, 2009

Heron, 2009
Jenni, 2008

Sheep, 2008

Seizure, 2009
Backyard, 2009

Plants, 2009

Conversation, 2009
White Pickup, 2009

Tortilla, 2009